I0841618

MY WIN OVER DEPRESSION

Author: TOMI B BAD

HOW TO USE THIS BOOK

When you need inspiration and help to move on, take this book in your hands and open it to any page without looking. Randomly. Read what it says slowly and concentrate on it. Read again if you want. Let it take you.

Then, create a positive thought in your mind. Anyone, it doesn't matter, as long as it's positive. Example: today is a beautiful day; the sun shines; my hands are clean; what a nice shirt; I'm going for a walk; I will make myself a coffee; what a beautiful car. And so on.

Then, take a pen, and to the right of the positive thought you read, write down your positive thinking on the blank page. It doesn't matter how, don't waste your time on nice handwriting. You can write from right to left, vice versa, from side to top, diagonally, and write it down in any script.

Then, read again what you wrote down and take a deep breath. Think only about that positive thought, let it fill you, and smile. If it helps, close your eyes. Smile.

Now close the book, put it somewhere close at hand, and go about your business. Start a new day. Start new ideas. Go to the job. Go to the girlfriend. Go anywhere, go. Move and don't stop.

And any time you feel the need, do it again. And again. As many times as necessary. Be persistent.

And you will feel the change.

Tomi B Bad

You must
sparkle the
change;
then, the
change puts
you on fire.

Do more of what makes you happy. Then, the happiness makes you do more.

You will face many defeats in life, but never let yourself be defeated.

Success is not final; failure is not fatal. It is the courage to continue that count.

No matter how you feel, get up, dress up, show up, and never give up.

I find that
the more I
try, the
more luck I
have.

The future belongs to those who believe in the future.

Winning
isn't
everything,
but wanting
to win is. Be
the one who
wants.

Whether you
think you
can or you
think you
can't, you're
right. So,
think you
can.

The most challenging thing is the decision to act; the rest is merely tenacity.

Dream big and dare to fail. But you will not fail today.

It does not matter how slowly you go as long as you do not stop.

Dreaming is a kind of planning. Dream a lot.

The fall is a flight, too. Don't be afraid to fly.

Be satisfied, not successful. Because others measure success, satisfaction is measured by you.

You will get nowhere by wishing it. You must act. Act now.

Every
journey
starts with
the first
step. Make
that step.

Don't
promise
when you're
happy. Don't
answer when
you're angry.
Don't decide
when you're
sad.

The secret of change is to focus all your energy not on fighting the old but on building the new.

If you can't fly, then run. If you can't run, then walk. But whatever you do, just keep moving.

Don't let rejection create self-doubt. Let it create character.

To build a
house, you
must dig a
hole for the
foundation.
So first you
go down to
get up.

Life is
never fair,
but it
always is
beautiful.

It is during
our darkest
moments
that we
must try to
see the light.

Pain is temporary. If you quit, however, it lasts forever.

Keep smiling. When it hurts the most, just keep smiling.

The road to success is paved with failures. Love your failures.

Life is 10% about what happens to you and 90% about how you react to it. Keep smiling.

Success without a failure is like pica without the chees.

Nothing is impossible; the word itself says, "I'm possible"!

To love yourself is the beginning of a lifelong romance.

The time you enjoy wasting is not a wasted time.

Being happy never goes out of style. Be stylish.

Sometimes, when things fall apart, they may actually fall into place.

A dead end is just an excellent place to turn around.

Even
miracles
take a little
time and a
little fate.

Failure is the condiment that gives success its flavor.

Everybody
has an
opinion
about how
you live your
life. Luckily,
you don't
have to care.

Don't bother
to be better
than your
neighbor.
Try to be
better than
yourself.

Mastering others is strength. Mastering yourself is might. Be mighty.

It is not the strength of the body that counts, but the strength of the spirit.

It's your life; you don't need someone's permission to live it.

The difference between winning and losing is most often not quitting.

When a new day begins, dare to smile. As it goes by, smile more.

If everything were perfect, you would never learn.

So, you're afraid? Be afraid. Be scared to the point you're trembling, but do it anyway!

We don't develop courage by being happy every day. We develop it by surviving difficult times.

Only success does not require an explanation. Quit explaining.

Scared is
what you're
feeling.
Brave is
what you're
doing. Be
brave.

The word "happy" would lose its meaning if there were no sadness. You would be sad before happy.

You are not what happened to you. You are what followed.

Knowing
others is
wisdom.
Knowing
yourself is
enlightenme
nt. Be sure to
bright every
day.

Smile in the mirror. Do that every morning, and you'll start to see a change.

A great
attitude is
like a
cookie. It is
always
welcome.
And you can
always have
some.

You are not
fully dressed
until you
wear a smile.
Be sharply
dressed.

The secret of getting ahead is getting started.

You have brains in your head. You have feet in your shoes. You can steer yourself in any direction you choose.

Just pick a
goal and
stick to it;
there are no
big,
complicated
secrets.

Do not fear failure. Dare to fail in order to find ways to succeed.

Just for the
record; not
all positive
change feels
positive in
the
beginning.
Be
persistent.

Once you
face your
fear, nothing
is ever as
hard as you
think. Do it
twice and
make a habit.

I have not
failed. I've
just found
10,000 ways
that won't
work before
1 that does.

You don't always need a plan. Sometimes, you just need to breathe, let go, and see what happens.

Real change, enduring change, happens one step at a time. Make that step.

You generate fears while we sit. You overcome them by standing up.

You have to
be where
you are to
get where
you need to
go. One step
at a time.

Definitions
belong to
the definers,
not the
defined.
Don't let
anyone
define you.

In order for
the light to
shine so
brightly, the
darkness
must be
present. Step
into the light
and shine.

Often, the small steps, not the giant leaps, bring the most lasting change. Make that step.

You're braver than you believe, stronger than you seem, and smarter than you think.

Tough times never last, but tough people do. You can be tough.

Believe you can, and you're halfway there.

Life isn't a
matter of
milestones
but of
moments.
Use this
moment.

Courage doesn't always roar. Sometimes courage is a quiet voice saying let's try again.

What you do
makes a
difference,
and you
decide what
kind of
difference
you want to
make.

Doubt is an enemy. Don't doubt yourself, just make one more effort.

Rivers know this: there is no hurry. We shall get there. Just move.

The purpose
of our lives
is to be
happy. So,
find a way to
be happy.

Life is a
series of
baby steps.
Slow,
unsteady,
small, but
get you
going.

The best
time for a
new
beginning is
now. Just
make a step.

A diamond is a chunk of coal that did well under pressure. So, you're on the path to shine.

Discourageme
nt and failure
are two of
the surest
stepping
stones to
success.

Nothing in the world can take the place of Persistence. One more step. And one more.

He who
conquers
himself is
the
mightiest
warrior.

Success comes when stumbling from failure to failure without loss of persistence.

Do the best
you can and
be happy
with it. No
one can do
more than
that.

You stood on
a mountain
of no's for
one yes. One
yes is often
all you need.

Failure is simply the opportunity to begin again, this time differently.

Our greatest glory is not in never falling but in rising every time we fall.

Start where
you are. Use
what you
have. Do
what you
can, no
matter how
small.